THE
WEAVER'S
LOST ART

[For a list of books published under the auspices of the
WORKING GROUP ON ISLAMISM AND THE INTERNATIONAL ORDER,
please see page 63.]

THE
WEAVER'S
LOST ART

Charles Hill

HOOVER INSTITUTION PRESS
Stanford University   Stanford, California

www.hoover.org

Hoover Institution Press Publication No. 650

Hoover Institution at Leland Stanford Junior University, Stanford, California, 94305-6010

First printing 2014
21 20 19 18 17 16 15 14   9 8 7 6 5 4 3 2 1

Manufactured in the United States of America

The paper used in this publication meets the minimum requirements of the American National Standard for Information Sciences— Permanence of Paper for Printed Library Materials, ANSI/NISO Z39.48-1992. ♾

Cataloging-in-Publication Data is available from the Library of Congress.
ISBN 978-0-8179-1765-4 (pbk.: alk. paper)
ISBN 978-0-8179-1766-1 (epub)
ISBN 978-0-8179-1767-8 (mobi)
ISBN 978-0-8179-1768-6 (PDF)

*The Hoover Institution gratefully acknowledges
the following individuals and foundations
for their significant support of the*

HERBERT AND JANE DWIGHT WORKING GROUP
ON ISLAMISM AND THE INTERNATIONAL ORDER:

Herbert and Jane Dwight

Mr. and Mrs. Norman R. Beall

Stephen Bechtel Foundation

Lynde and Harry Bradley Foundation

Mr. and Mrs. Clayton W. Frye Jr.

Lakeside Foundation

CONTENTS

The Great Unraveling:
The Remaking of the Middle East

IT'S A MANTRA, but it is also true: the Middle East is being unmade and remade. The autocracies that gave so many of these states the appearance of stability are gone, their dreaded rulers dispatched to prison or exile or cut down by young people who had yearned for the end of the despotisms. These autocracies were large prisons, and in 2011, a storm overtook that stagnant world. The spectacle wasn't pretty, but prison riots never are. In the Fertile Crescent, the work of the colonial cartographers—Gertrude Bell, Winston Churchill, and Georges Clemenceau— are in play as they have never been before. Arab nationalists were given to lamenting that they lived in nation-states "invented" by Western powers in the aftermath of the Great War. Now, a century later, with the ground burning in Lebanon, Syria, and Iraq and the religious sects at war, not even the most ardent nationalists can be sure that they can put in place anything better than the old order.

Men get used to the troubles they know, and the Greater Middle East seems fated for grief and breakdown. Outside powers approach it with dread; merciless political contenders have the run of it. There is swagger in Iran and a belief that the radical theocracy can bully its rivals into submission. There was a period when the United States provided a modicum of order in these Middle Eastern lands. But pleading fatigue, and financial scarcity at home, we have all but announced the end of that stewardship. We are poorer for that abdication, and the Middle East is thus left to the mercy of predators of every kind.

We asked a number of authors to give this spectacle of disorder their best try. We imposed no rules on them, as we were sure their essays would take us close to the sources of the malady.

FOUAD AJAMI
Senior Fellow, Hoover Institution—
Cochairman, Herbert and Jane Dwight Working Group
on Islamism and the International Order

CHARLES HILL
Distinguished Fellow of the Brady-Johnson Program
in Grand Strategy at Yale University;
Research Fellow, Hoover Institution—
Cochairman, Herbert and Jane Dwight Working Group
on Islamism and the International Order

The Weaver's Lost Art

CHARLES HILL

THE TANGLED SKEIN of the world's problems is Gordian knotted in the worst places; in other words, what we call the field of international relations—global studies, foreign affairs, world politics, etc.—in recent years has evolved into one more dimension of professional policy analysis or social science research, as the methodologies of domestic issues are applied with scant success to the larger outside scene.

But there has always been something mysterious and intellectually profound hovering around such matters, something now disdained or forgotten. Hegel conveyed the sense that here, in high world affairs, lay the most significant philosophical and moral questions of the human

1

condition, questions which, if not ultimately answerable, had to be confronted if humanity were to grasp its own meaning. This in turn implied that ideas and assumptions of the greatest consequence might be at work far below the surface of strategy, policy, and daily operations. This essay will attempt to locate and illuminate that realm.

For a hundred years or more the United States has acted as the monitor and guarantor of the international state system and the elemental requirements of world order, sometimes intervening, sometimes standing aside, sometimes deferring to the United Nations and the claims of international law. Now, in the early twenty-first century, it appears that the US is abdicating, no longer willing—and soon perhaps no longer able—to take a leading responsibility for the maintenance of international peace and security.

Why do nations do what they do? And why do they cease to do so? The source of the traditional American approach to the world has been religion transposed or reconstituted as national strategic interest. When religion as a felt underlying force evaporates, the national strategic interest dries up as well.

A core debate about the meaning of the modern age is whether contemporary political thought is legitimately innovative or whether it is a secularized, sanitized version of religion or premodern beliefs. As the 1648 Treaty of Westphalia, which originated the modern international system, relegated religion to the sidelines of world affairs and because modernization was declared by Max Weber to progressively erase modern man's desire for the spiritual, the outcome of the debate is consequential. Put simply, the German-Jewish philosopher Karl Löwith argued that modernity's commitment to social perfection through national policy has in fact been a disguised version of the belief in eternal salvation through revelation. The German philosopher Hans Blumenberg rebutted Löwith by declaring that the scientific revolution has been intellectually authentic, an advance on an idea that was encompassed by medieval philosophy: nominalism, or the need to grasp the physical workings of *this* world. So modern scientific developments should not be regarded as a disguised form of premodern spiritual belief.

Although not taking a position on the Löwith-Blumenberg "Legitimacy of the Modern Age" debate, the inescapable conclusion is that the US role in the world across the decades of the twentieth century cannot be understood without awareness of its religious sources and inclinations.

Fouad Ajami, with his perspicacious sense for the clarifying characterization, has called this moment "the Great Unraveling," the perfect phase for the art of statecraft in our time, especially in the Middle East.

THE GREAT METAPHOR

Since remote antiquity, statecraft's great metaphor has been weaving. Traces of cloth found at Fayoum and depictions of weavers at work on the walls of pharaonic Egypt reveal the centrality of weaving to ordered life in the ancient world.

The Parthenon frieze displays the annual Panathenaic procession. There, amid powerful horses and straining warriors appear young girls carrying a newly woven cloth—the *peplos*—for robing the statue of Athena, a ceremony central to Athens's image of itself as a polis or state. To underline this, Plato's dialogue *Statesman* explicitly designates weaving as expressing the statesman's role—helped by the orator, the general, and the judge, whose arts though distinct from statesmanship are akin to it. The challenge is to weave the aggressive and courageous warp of society to the contained and self-controlled weft.[1]

The fey delights of Shakespeare's *A Midsummer Night's Dream* mask its grand strategic context: the political and cultural enigma posed by the looming succession crisis produced by Queen Elizabeth's evasion of every attempt to urge her into a dynastic marriage. In this sense, Elizabeth was following the strategy of Penelope in Homer's *Odyssey,* unweaving every evening the fabric that she had produced during the day. In the play, Bottom the weaver—he of the donkey's head and human body—is a weaver in the

---

1. Arlene W. Saxonhouse, review of Lisa Pace Vetter, *Women's Work as Political Art: Weaving and Dialectical Politics in Homer, Aristophanes, and Plato.* Rowman & Littlefield, 2005, in *Perspectives on Politics*, 4, no. 2 (June 2006): 371–2.

strategic sense, intertwining the fairy realm with the real world and commoners with the nobility, a wise fool capable of playing and integrating all the theatrical parts.

For America, the great metaphor of weaving is made powerfully central to strategic consciousness through Herman Melville's *Moby-Dick*—in the chapter "Moby-Dick"—by a strange reference to the Hotel de Cluny, the fifteenth-century house of the Abbott of Cluny, built on the ruins of Roman thermal baths, themselves built on earlier, primeval foundations—down and down in time and space and thought where may be discovered "the old State-secret," suggesting that statecraft has roots reaching down to the origins of the political community.

On a cloudy, sultry, lazy day, Ishmael and Queequeg are mildly employed in weaving a large mat of the sort ships require to protect their beam sides from clashing against docks or other ships. Ishmael says:

> As I kept passing and repassing the filling or wool of marline between the long yarns of the warp, using my own hand for the shut-

tle, and as Queequeg, standing sideways, ever and anon slid his heavy oaken sword between the threads, and idly looking off upon the water, carelessly and unthinkingly drove home every yarn . . . it seemed to me as if this were the Loom of Time.

Ishmael explains the factors at work are the straight warp of *necessity; chance* (though restrained in its play between the lines of *necessity*); and *free will* "plying her shuttle between given threads." The shuttle, or sword, carries the thread across the loom in order to weave the weft with the warp.

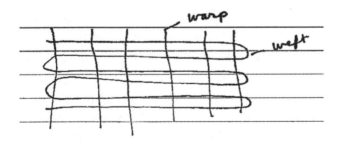

That we are invited to consider this as a profound metaphor for the management of the human condition becomes clear. The ways of the world are "as a weaver's loom," and the supreme "weaver-god, he weaves." As an epic, *Moby-Dick* must have an invocation. Uniquely it is to the weaver-god as "the centre and circumference of all *democracy!*"

We may say that in the international system *states* are the warp, the necessary foundation of the system. *Regimes,* or governments, are the weft, somewhat constrained within the four corners of the state but able by chance of circumstance to shape the directions and purposes of the polity. And free will is the shuttle that is plied in and around the composition through policy-making decisions and the use of force and craft (i.e., diplomacy) in tandem. The missing element in the modern, Westphalian international state system—or perhaps the stroke of genius that has made it universally acceptable—is that it matters not what kind of regime governs the state. In *Moby-Dick* the regime that the weaver-god intends is democracy, but that political form, in Melville's time, is distinctively American and not yet acceptable to the world at large.

Melville's *Moby-Dick* is a manual for statecraft, at least for American statecraft; it contains and is surrounded by references to the Middle East as the Holy Land, references that point back and forward in time and which provide both a duty to maintain world order and the necessity for a leader capable of making decisions, all materials for the work of weaving.

Among the Middle East factors in and around the epic are these: while *Moby-Dick* was being written, there took place the extraordinary 1848 United States Navy expedition down the Jordan River to the Dead Sea under the command of Lt. William F. Lynch, whose mission had nothing to do with naval or international security matters but was to try to locate the biblical sites of Sodom and Gomorrah. The central consciousness of the book is Ishmael, whose name recalls the child of Abraham and Hagar and who is considered the ancestor of the Arab people. At the end of the work, when the *Pequod* and its crew are lost, Ishmael is rescued by the ship *Rachel,* namesake of the mother of the Jewish people. And of course there is the biblically named Captain Ahab, who transformed the purpose of the voyage from commercial whaling to a monomaniacal metaphysical quest when he nailed a doubloon to the mast. Starbuck, the ship's leading Christian, envisions the Trinity in the coin's engraved surface; but for others it is a golden calf, spreading confusion. As the novel ends, with Ishmael clinging in the sea to Queequeg's coffin, "the old State-secret" remains unrecognized, unpracticed. Ishmael will survive to write the epic book about it, a work that will go far beyond the measuring of bones that he once thought might explain the mystery of the white whale. Ahab the captain has gone to the ocean depths bound to Moby-Dick. America still awaited its statesman.

There is a long foreground to this, reaching to the origins of the American psyche, character, and polity.

No key unlocks the meaning of *Moby-Dick;* as one of the greatest works of literature, it leaves all interpreters floundering in its wake. But one image is unmistakably clear: the *Pequod* is the American ship of state, with its 30-man crew— 30 states at that time—drawn from every imaginable racial, religious, linguistic, and geographic place and people. It is a voyage that imagines its purpose as all things to all men. For our Middle Eastern interests, it self-defines America as uniquely able to hold the trust and play the statesman's role for Arabs and Jews alike. That moment would not come until the mid-twentieth century.

After *Moby-Dick* was published and largely ignored, Melville made a personal expedition to the Holy Land in the hope, not to be realized, of finding answers to his doubts about religious faith. This he would chronicle in "Clarel: A Poem and Pilgrimage to the Holy Land" in 1876. Longer than "Paradise Lost" and just as much a journey through biblical texts, "Clarel" like *Moby-Dick,* but with more reason, was also ignored.

Moby-Dick's, and Melville's, obsession with Palestine was a central contribution to the definition of American identity both before and after the Civil War. But the strategy the United States followed through the nineteenth century was not designed for shaping world order; it was a mission to "bring in the sheaves" of souls for the next world.

In graduate school I was on an architectural history team commissioned to advise the US government on how to convert Robert Mills's— the architect of the Washington Monument— Old Patent Office Building into the National Portrait Gallery. The final task was to recommend notable Americans to be selected for display. We quickly realized that if we chose those then regarded as in the forefront of nineteenth-century American society, almost all of them would be clergymen; most of those we today think of as important would not appear.

America's approach to the world of that time was to deploy missionaries to bring about "the evangelization of the world in this generation." The American Board of Commissioners for Foreign Missions sent its first missionaries to the Middle East, to Smyrna, in 1819. As one scholar observed, "If the Puritans in the seventeenth century projected biblical landscapes onto American landscapes, in the nineteenth century the opposite possibility arose: to redefine America's biblical heritage through the landscape of Palestine."[2] The first priority was the conversion of Jews, then Muslims, and in doing so to supplant Catholicism in the region; soon would come the shock of recognition that such objectives were wildly beyond reach. American missionaries would then turn to a process of serving all the populations of the Middle East, with conversion attempts giving way to providing medicine and schooling.

Yet in the course of this great missionary century, two strategic realities did shape the views of Americans and those they encountered around the world. First, the missionaries were closely involved with US officials: the US Navy protected them and carried foreign service officers to support American interests diplomatically. In one region after another, missionaries not only represented but also were the US to the local population. Second, the American involvement was universal, worldwide in range and inclusive of the variety of people encountered. China was the other chief focus of the endeavor,

2. Ilana Pardes, *Melville's Bibles* (Berkeley: University of California Press, 2008), 76.

as powerfully described in Pearl S. Buck's story of her missionary father, *Fighting Angel,* and John Hersey's sprawling novel *The Call.* The end of the American missionary century was symbolically marked by the murder of Horace Tracy Pitkin at Pao-ting-fu near Peking during the 1900 Boxer Rebellion; but the residue of the cause, transformed by international security concerns, would be recognizable in the US Navy's gunboat years on the Yangtze River in the 1920s.

As seen by a leading historian of religion in American war and diplomacy, Andrew Preston, the spiritual causes of the nineteenth century were transposed for the early twentieth century into a series of crusades, the first being the Spanish-American War as shaped by the international lawyer Elihu Root, who was bred in New York state's "burned-over (by evangelism) district"; Alfred Thayer Mahan, for whom religion was indispensable; and the "muscular Christianity" of Theodore Roosevelt declaring that "We stand at Armageddon and we battle for the Lord." The Philippines, acquired in the war, had to be remade by Protestants "in our

(American) image" but, in a commitment to universalism, preserving the role of Catholicism while separating church and state. William Howard Taft went to the Vatican to consult and emerged with the praise of Pope Leo XIII.

President Woodrow Wilson would represent the nineteenth-century American missionary transformed into a twentieth-century world strategic leader. Wilson's earliest and closest biographer, Arthur Link, described the leader:

> Not only a man of ideas; he was, even more importantly, a citizen of another invisible world, the world of the spirit in which a sovereign God reigned in justice and in love. . . . Born the son of a Presbyterian minister and a devout mother and reared in the southern Presbyterian church, he absorbed completely his Father's and his denomination's belief in the omnipotence of God, the morality of the universe, a system of rewards and punishments, and the supreme revelation of Jesus Christ. Mankind, he felt, lived not only by the providence of God but also under his immutable

decrees; and nations as well as men transgressed the divine ordinance at their peril. He shared the Calvinistic belief . . . in predestination, the absolute conviction that God had ordered the universe from the beginning, the Faith that God used men for his own purposes. From such beliefs came a sure sense of destiny and a feeling of intimate connection with the source of power.

Wilson's 1917 declaration of war was at odds with key American religious leaders, but out of it came the first-ever idealistic synthesis, a grouping identifiable as America's first-ever liberal internationalists: a fusion of Protestants, Catholics, and Jews, and hawks and doves alike. Although Wilson did not take the US into war for a specifically religious reason, it would be "a war for the good of the world to ensure perpetual peace." The significant point was that, as a Christian nation, the US was obligated to assume the mantle of leadership. Wilson's world-acclaimed "Fourteen Points" were founded on Christianity's Golden Rule. It was not by chance, Preston notes, that the League of Nations was called a covenant at Wilson's insistence, in the lineage of the Scottish Covenanters of the 1630s, and headquartered in the birthplace of Calvinism, Geneva.

Franklin Delano Roosevelt would next embody the country's civic religion as the first president to prioritize faith as the essence of democracy. FDR was not a reader of *Moby-Dick,* but his statecraft exemplified the epic novel's recognition of a divine force as both the Great Weaver and the Great Democrat. Roosevelt, who could tolerate all faiths but not a lack of faith, codified religion in US foreign policy and explained World War II as a struggle for religious liberty. Again and again Roosevelt instructed his aides when facing a complex problem to "weave things together."

Across the early to mid-twentieth-century, as American religion was being transfigured into American international security strategy and the country involved itself in three foreign wars, Christian pacifism was energized into opposition. A compelling new theological thinker, Reinhold Niebuhr, seemed to argue for a vigorous US role in managing the dangers of world affairs. The only Christian doctrine that had been empirically demonstrated, Niebuhr sardonically declared, was original sin. In Niebuhr's Lutheran background one could imagine hearing that sixteenth-century Augustinian monk conveying the words of Saint Augustine on the need for a temporal leader to take "*severe* decisions" if this fallen world were not to collapse in total disaster.

But in *The Irony of American History,* published in 1952, in the context of the new age of nuclear weapons, Niebuhr put forward a stinging rebuke to America's role of world leadership, fulminating against "our dreams of managing history." From the earliest New England Puritan years, Niebuhr declared, there has been a "deep layer of messianic consciousness in the mind of America—not immune to the temptation of believing that the universal validity of what we held in trust justified our own use of power to establish it." So, he concluded, "the progress of American culture toward hegemony in the world community as well as toward the ultimate in standards of living has brought us everywhere to limits where our ideals and norms are brought under ironic indictment." As an example, in his book, Niebuhr sneered at American support for transforming post–World War II Japan from an empire into a democracy.

Yet this was the same Niebuhr who famously said, "Man's capacity for justice makes democracy possible; but man's inclination to injustice makes democracy necessary." Is this fence-straddling, ambiguity, or realistic wisdom? A pacifist who supported America's entrance into the Second World War and saw the need to oppose godless communism also spoke of moral equivalency. "We are more like our enemies than we think," he wrote, for there is "an ironic consensus between two apparently antithetical giants" suggesting the Cold War was a needless concoction of two similarly problematic and immature societies. Yet, at the same time, Niebuhr quoted George F. Kennan's call to make America's national interest the touchstone of US diplomacy in order to declare Kennan wrong: "For egotism is not the proper cure for abstract and pretentious idealism. . . . A preoccupation with our own interests must lead to an illegitimate indifference toward the interest of others, even when modesty prompts the preoccupation."

In short, Niebuhr—the darling of interventionists and isolationists alike, but never at the same time—is infuriating as a guide. But to be Niebuhrian about Niebuhr, therein may reside his enduring value: our world is a fallen world, beset by original sin; therefore, a prince is needed to take hard decisions—including the use of force that would be immoral if employed by an ordinary person—in order to maintain at least rudimentary stability and security for humankind. But such a prince and his government must never forget that they, too, are beset by original sin, and pull back from the arrogance and aggressiveness that innately are generated by the employment of forceful means.

This is not a bad way to assess American foreign and defense policy across the Cold War with its most memorable markers steeped in religious meanings: President Harry S. Truman expressing his Baptist beliefs in recognizing Israel, the captivity of Cardinal Mindszenty, the moral agonizings of John Foster Dulles, the words "under God" added to the Pledge of

Allegiance, the National Prayer Breakfast, and Catholic support for Ngo Dinh Diem in Vietnam. They all played out against the background of the Reverend Billy Graham's unflagging support for every president even as a coalition of pastors, priests, and other religious leaders clamored for peace, dialogue, disarmament, and concessions to all adversaries. Mainline Protestantism would not survive such internal tensions.

"THE OLD STATE-SECRET" AND THE MIDDLE EAST

The Middle East seemed to offer no handhold for serious American diplomacy until the late 1960s, when an Arab-Israeli war's outcome created possibilities for a statecraft of "weaving."

The 1967 war gave diplomacy "something to work with," an awareness that there now were several strands that might be interwoven. First, Israel was seeking peace and recognition while the Arabs were seeking to regain territory lost in the fighting. This became the basis of the unanimously passed UN Security Council Resolution 242, the only international legal document to—eventually—be accepted by all parties. In it, "the states concerned" called for an Arab-Israel trade-off: territory for peace. Israel would withdraw from lands taken in the war and in return would gain recognition, security, and peace from the Arabs.

Second, a deep-rooted cultural difference was observable: the Arab side insisted, for reasons of "honor," that any solution to the conflict must be "comprehensive," with all issues resolved at once in one major agreement. In stark contrast, the Israelis considered progress to be impossible unless it was made step-by-step with each step capable of providing a stable platform of trust for the next. After all, this was how the modern state of Israel had been achieved: "goat by goat; dunam by dunam"—a dunam being an Ottoman-era unit of land that could be plowed in a day.

Third, this led to one of the most impressive examples of weaving in diplomatic history, the Camp David Accords of 1978, in which state-to-state negotiations between Egypt and Israel aimed at a treaty of peace—a traditional form of diplomacy—would be interlinear with the new reality of a non-state party, the Palestine Liberation Organization, for which little or no precedent existed in classic diplomatic practice. To put them together the accords fashioned a new concept. Egypt would negotiate on behalf of the Palestinians as the state partner across the table from the state of Israel, it being understood that traditional diplomatic practice, UN Security Council Resolution 242, as a product of "the states concerned" and the realities of world politics all required that treaties be made between member states of the international system. "The old State-secret" of weaving was here carried out on the loom of another old necessity: a prince with the required capability to take "severe decisions," as demonstrated by Egyptian President Anwar Sadat's decision to go to Jerusalem and Menachem Begin's decision to give up the Sinai and open a process with the Palestinians. Saint Augustine's recognition of the indispensable role of such a prince in the cause of world order was not to be confined to one religion alone.

A fourth factor—time—was also woven into the design as work on an Egypt-Israel treaty of peace meant to stand the test of time was interspersed with the concept of Israeli-Palestinian arrangements, each of which would be tested on a limited basis to determine whether it could be institutionalized or put on the shelf for the time being.

The interweaving of such multilevel, multi-conceptual factors was disrupted when the warp—the state factor—was ripped out of the loom. When Sadat was assassinated in 1981 and the Arab states—and the United Nations—rejected the treaty of peace, Egypt dropped out of its role as state negotiator for the Palestinians. King Hussein then came forward to offer the Hashemite kingdom of Jordan to fill the state role. But under rejectionist Arab pressure Jordan soon turned away from that responsibility. Although efforts were made to keep the peace process going, from that point forward it was a futile undertaking. High hopes were raised by other approaches taken in Madrid, Oslo, Geneva, and elsewhere, but none could meet the fundamental requirements for the weaver's art. A back-channel "track two" effort in the 1990s under the guidance of former Secretary of State George P. Shultz aimed at replacing the missing state negotiator piece by an initiative given the label "makloubeh"—an Arabic dish cooked upside down—which would provide for Palestinian statehood first rather than at the end of the process so the Palestinians could be their own state negotiator.

This back-channel idea aroused a surprising level of interest on the Israeli side, but it died with the outbreak of the second intifada in 2000.

The wrecking of the Arab-Israeli peace process called to mind the nineteenth-century Luddites in England, who, aggrieved by the industrialization of wool-making, set out to destroy the looms—and their own futures—altogether.

This destruction was compounded in the late twentieth and early twenty-first century by Islamists, whose religiously driven ideology rejected the international state system in its entirety and who were able, through intimidation, fear, and theocratic condemnation, to spread their destructive demands to leading sectors in Muslim states. The Egypt-Israel state-to-state relationship and peace treaty and the Camp David structure for advancing toward a two-state solution—the state of Israel and a to-be-formed state of Palestine—were anathema to the Islamists; nothing could be a greater setback to their cause than the creation of a state of Palestine; the Islamists' successful assault on Middle East diplomacy was an immense achievement for them and a severe blow to the international state system.

Meanwhile, a monumental Islamist achievement took place: the 1979 revolution in Iran of Ayatollah Ruhollah Khomeini, which would uniquely place the first anti-international system and radically religion-driven movement in charge of a legitimate, sovereign state—Iran— inside the established world order. This truly was a case of the enemy now well entrenched inside the walls. A revolutionary force, by definition, aims to oppose the established international system at every turn, to tear down the status quo and replace it with the revolution's own adversarial concept of world order. This the Islamic Republic of Iran has done. Tellingly, its first-world-shaking act was directed at the international state system's most basic mechanism for comity among states: diplomatic immunity, as Iranian revolutionaries stormed the US Embassy in Tehran to seize

American personnel and hold them hostage for 444 days.

Islamist Iran then proceeded deftly to weave its own pattern of statecraft: its warp would be to employ the privileges and immunities of its newly gained statehood against the state system when it served Iran's interests; its weft would be to use the outlawed methods of revolution against the state system when that angle of approach would best serve the interests of the ayatollah's regime. Over the next 25 years revolutionary Iran would weave its version of hegemonic, radical Shia rule over the entire region even as it manipulated the established protocols and assumptions of traditional diplomacy against their intended purpose. Thus in the first decade of the twenty-first century, Iran could emerge as an accepted state in the international system in possession of a nuclear-weapons capability, which it had gained by violating international law to the extent of disabling the Nuclear Nonproliferation Treaty—and all the while continuing to operate as a terrorist-supporting state aimed at the destabilization of other states in the region and beyond.

THE PRINCE

If "the old State-secret" is the art of weaving carried to high world-political situations, history reveals that the technique of weaving can be used for good or ill. The secret will be known and employed by the most astute among leaders—or it may be the quality that differentiates dictators and autocrats from "statesmen." Modern world affairs has been a struggle between statesmen with an awareness, perhaps innate, of weaving as a way to *manage* the world's problems, say Prince Metternich with his weave of congresses "taking the shape of a Cabinet of the Great Powers" as opposed to powerful figures who intend to impose themselves on the world in order to *shape* it to their will, as attempted by Napoleon.

A look at the ancient world, biblical and classical, suggests the line between strategy and grand strategy may be determined by whether statecraft involves weaving or not. Moses was a grand strategist but the Hebrew Bible is bereft of strategic weaving, and the New Testament has none—unless one considers the synoptic gospels taken together as a woven product. Jesus was not a grand strategist, but Paul through his physical travels, written Epistles, and taut systems of thought was surely engaged in creating an immense tapestry of conviction and conduct. Without Paul there would have been Christians but no Christianity. Paul's weave displays how a Christian community works and what it signifies: "love, participation, indwelling bind all together."[3] Starting out as a tent maker, Paul knew the practical art of weaving animal hair into a protective shelter for people.

For the classical world as well, the assessment scale reveals grand strategy to be rare and difficult to achieve. Herodotus's telling of the battles of Marathon, Thermopylae, and Salamis can be understood as a single three-act drama of a nation's instinctive self-organization as it begins to recognize that "the free fight better," that unity is imperative, and that national character can be a strategic instrument. Thucydides's Peloponnesian War history conveys to close

---

3. Diarmaid MacCulloch, *Christianity: The First Three Thousand Years* (New York: Viking Press, 2010), 106.

readers that Pericles was a statesman but not a grand strategist, part of the polity's problem with democratic deterioration rather than a bulwark against it.

Rome's great historians Polybius, Livy, and Tacitus depict the transformation from republican virtue to imperial vainglory and debauchery. In the process, however, Virgil provided a model for weaving—the multifariously integrated necessities of farming and animal husbandry as read to Augustus from the poet's "Georgics" and then, in the "Aeneid," the first great message of the statesman as one who must order the world in peace. Aeneas, who fled from burning Troy, knew that his destiny was to found a new nation, but he knew not why or wherefore until he went to the underworld, where he was instructed by the shade of Anchises, his father:

> Other people will, I do not doubt, still cast
> their bronze to breathe with softer features,
> or draw out of the marble living lines, plead
> causes better, trace the ways of heaven with
> wounds and tell the rising constellations;

but yours will be the rulership of nations; remember, Roman, these will be your arts: to teach the ways of peace to those you conquer, to spare defeated peoples, tame the proud. ("Aeneid," book VI, p. 853–881)

Or, in simpler terms, to crown peace with civilization. The "Aeneid" envisions a Rome that interweaves divine substance and imperial theology—to bring peace on earth, with Caesar Augustus as the Prince of Peace.

The mutual effect of pagan imperial Rome and nascent Christianity is among humanity's most consequential yet still not fully explained interactions. The former Pope Benedict XVI, in his *Jesus of Nazareth: The Infancy Narratives,* argues that when the Gospel of Luke describes Jesus's birth in the context of the Augustan empire, as Joseph and Mary must go to Bethlehem to register for taxation, it compels a comparison between one prince of peace and another—Augustus, the *Princeps Pacis* and *Pontifex Maximus.* The epithet was more than propaganda, Benedict says. "It expressed a heartfelt longing in the people of the time, wracked by the Roman civil wars and conflicts between the Roman Empire and her rivals to the east. We may see how seriously it was taken by studying Augustus's Altar of Peace (*Ara Pacis*) in Rome, consecrated a few years before Jesus's birth. It was so placed, says the Pope, that on the emperor's birthday, between morning and evening, the sun cast the shadow of an obelisk along a line that struck the very center of the altar, where Augustus himself was portrayed as supreme pontiff."[4] So Christianity, through Paul, produces a grand strategy to challenge Augustus's grand strategy, which was itself produced in emulation of Virgil's woven words.

Thus may be formed a hypothesis on how a major concept took shape over centuries.

Augustine's *City of God*, begun in AD 410 as Alaric's Goths were sacking Rome, developed over the thirteen years of its writing into a manual for Christianity's grand strategic management of the empire. Saint Paul, in Romans Chapter 13, already "had given authoritative support to a positive evaluation of government as a

---

4. Anthony Esolen, review of Joseph Ratzinger (Pope Benedict XVI), *Jesus of Nazareth: The Infancy Narratives*. Image Books, 2012, in the *Wall Street Journal*, December 17, 2012, p. A16.

providential instrument of order."[5] As the result of Adam's fall, this was a fallen world beset by constant distress and upheaval. Basic order would have to be maintained so that people could focus their lives and souls on the ordered world other than this world: the City of God. So a Christian prince was needed to take the "severe decisions" required to, as it would be put centuries later, "maintain international peace and security." In retelling the biblical story, Augustine would also provide a metahistory for the world, casting aside the classical world's conception of cyclical, or seasonal, time and installing linear time, which had a starting point, direction, and purpose—in other words, the idea of progress.

The *City of God* story line would become, over a thousand years later, the scaffolding for John Milton's "Paradise Lost." Milton served as diplomatic and Hebrew language secretary to Oliver Cromwell in the Puritan Revolution, and Cromwell could be seen as an exemplar of the

---

5. Henry Chadwick, *Augustine* (Oxford & New York: Oxford University Press, 1988), 100.

severe-decision-taking prince in the sense envisioned by Augustine:

> A careful reading of his letters and speeches shows that Cromwell believed that it was for the purpose of winning ordered Christian liberty that the Parliamentary soldiers took up their arms.[6]

The objective, therefore, was not to impose Puritanism on others but to advance the cause of world order. From classical to early modern times, the concept of a *translatio studii et imperii* was felt, the supposedly inexorable movement of imperial power and learning from East (i.e., Troy) to West. "Westward the course of empire takes its way," said Bishop Berkeley, he who gave his name to Berkeley College at Yale and Berkeley, California.

Then suddenly Cromwell was dead and the revolution of the saints collapsed. The three Puritan judges who had sentenced King Charles I to

---

6. Maurice Ashley, *The Greatness of Oliver Cromwell* (London & New York: Macmillan Company, 1958), 364.

death in 1649 fled to hide in a cave near New Haven, Connecticut. One day in 1993, while looking through the upper rooms of an abandoned Yale secret society building that had been taken over by the university, I found in what would have been the delegation's gathering room an engraving of Cromwell, lying facedown in the dust. Cromwell's cause had failed in England, but his name and fame had taken hold in New England, where leafy streets were given the names of Puritan battle victories and a town would call itself Cromwell.

So there came to America the concept of a prince-in-arms inspired by an other-wordly faith and dedicated to the order of this world, as described by Augustine:

If they are slow to punish, but ready to
 pardon;
If they take vengeance on wrong because
 of the necessity
To direct and protect the state, and not to
 satisfy
Their personal animosity; if they grant
 pardon not

To allow impunity to wrong-doing but in
    the hope
of amendment of the wrong-doer; if when
    they
are obliged to take severe decisions as
    must often
happen, they compensate this with the
    gentleness
of their mercy and the generosity of their
    benefits;
if they restrain their self-indulgent
    appetites all
the more because they are more free to
    gratify them,
and prefer to have command over their
    lower
desires than over any number of subject
    peoples;
and if they do all this not for a burning
    desire
for empty glory, but for the love of eternal
blessedness, and if they do not fail to offer to
their true God, as a sacrifice for their sins,
the oblation of humility, compassion, and
    prayer . . .

. . . then, it is leaders of this kind whom we
call happy.[7]

The ideal would never be attained, but, in a sacred or secular political form, it entered the American polity and its self-sense of purpose in and for the world.

Henry David Thoreau made the wrong call for the right reason when, obsessed with the antislavery movement, he "thought Brown all the time" to compare and call forward John Brown as the Cromwell America needed at the moment. Theodore Roosevelt wrote Cromwell's biography and studied his statecraft. And, as a boy, "Tommy" Woodrow Wilson "lay in the thick grass atop old Confederate ammunition bunkers and debated the sources of greatness in the incomparable Oliver Cromwell."[8]

For the Second World War the US produced FDR, the consummate weaver; for the Cold War, it was Truman who would take "severe decisions."

---

7. Augustine, Book V of *The City of God*, Ch. 24.
8. W. Barksdale Maynard, *Woodrow Wilson: Princeton to the Presidency* (New Haven: Yale University Press, 2008), 8.

THE UNRAVELING

When the Arab League took the required Arab state partner out of the Camp David peace process—and when the United Nations, in the most disgraceful act of its existence, refused to recognize the peace treaty or provide UN peace-keepers for the Sinai—no diplomacy toward a successful two-state outcome, Palestinian and Israeli, was possible.

The US then, under near impossible diplomatic disadvantages, began to try to strengthen or substitute for the elements needed to begin once more a weaving statecraft for the Middle East. From this angle of approach the 1982 Israel-PLO war in Lebanon was used, through the unique skills of America's Lebanon-born Ambassador Philip Habib and subsequently by Secretary of State Shultz, as a platform for reconstituting the independence and territorial integrity of the Lebanese state. Two parts of a four-dimensional effort succeeded. The US-negotiated May 17 agreement failed to get all foreign troops out of Lebanon, and President Ronald Reagan's September 1 initiative to relaunch the peace process was not accepted by the parties. But Habib's unceasing peace-making efforts, which hastened his death soon after, did rid Beirut of gangland-style dominance as Yasir Arafat was compelled to move his PLO lair to Tunis. And Shultz's personal campaign to enhance the Palestinians' quality of life and persuade the Israelis to turn away from their socialist inclinations strengthened the potential of each for productive statehood.

In the larger international arena, America's Cold War weave under Reagan was carried out in distinctive micro and macro forms. The US set a four-part agenda that it would unfailingly insist upon covering at every US-Soviet meeting: human rights, nuclear weapons, regional conflicts (with the Middle East uppermost), and consular issues. This constant thrumming beat was conducted, in an almost unconscious way, as what in retrospect resembled an interconnected ring composition, the literary structure used in Homeric antiquity to provide a message to the mind of the listener.

The composition began with rhetoric: Reagan's branding the Soviet Union an "evil empire"; then the buildup of US military strength; and then a major shift in doctrine: missile defense, a radical departure from deterrence. In Reagan's second term came another major doctrinal shift: American support for guerrilla freedom fighters, a departure from the doctrine of containment. This was accompanied by diplomatic engagement with the Russians on nuclear reduction. And finally back to rhetoric: "Tear down this wall!" It was a ring composition worthy of the "Iliad" and "Odyssey," with the two Cold War doctrines turned inside out at exactly the moment of greatest effect: deterrence and containment redefined to turn the tide of the global contest.

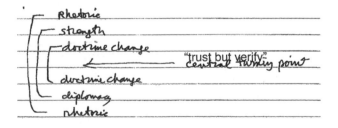

In a classic ring composition, the centerpiece usually holds the key: here it would be Reagan's "trust but verify" decision on the elimination of an entire class of nuclear weapons.

This newly woven tapestry did much to bring about the end of the Cold War and the collapse of the Soviet Union. The crumbling of Kremlin support put unprecedented pressure on the PLO, and the US moved quickly to capitalize on it. Secretary of State Shultz deftly oversaw a push-pull effort that produced from PLO leader Arafat—now bereft of Moscow's financial, political, and military backing—the "three yeses" that America required before a substantive dialogue could begin. Cornered in Geneva, Arafat accepted Israel's right to exist as a state, accepted UN Security Council Resolution 242, and renounced terrorism, even mentioning Israel's name.

At the same time a momentous "severe decision" was taken by President George H. W. Bush toward restoring integrity to the international state system in the Middle East. In 1990 Saddam Hussein, assuming that US fatigue from the end of the Cold War would allow him to get away with what in effect was an international murder, invaded Kuwait to simply erase that country as a state in the accepted sense, turning it into Iraq's nineteenth province. America then organized and led an international coalition force— Operation Desert Storm—to restore Kuwait's sovereignty as a member state of the United Nations, doing so on the foundation of a long line of UN Security Council resolutions designed to curb Saddam's depredations and his weapons of mass destruction.

A "FAILURE TO REALIZE" DECADE

But end-of-Cold War fatigue was setting in, and America's attention to world order flagged. Secretary of State James A. Baker III, superbly prepared and determined to practice a statecraft of the highest order, nonetheless let it be known that he intended to confine himself to three or four of the most significant challenges, a deviation from a classic statesman's awareness that everything counts. Baker also disbanded the State Department's experienced Middle East peace process team of foreign service officers, lawyers, and intelligence analysts and put the Israeli-Palestinian issue in the hands of only one official, an impossible assignment.

In September 1993 on the South Lawn of the White House, President Bill Clinton, Israeli Prime Minister Yitzhak Rabin, and PLO Chairman Arafat posed for the famous handshake photograph after they signed their declaration of principles based on an agreement unofficially negotiated at Oslo. The media and much of the world were thrilled by the scene, not realizing that the absence of an Arab state partner to the agreement doomed it from the start.

Earlier in 1993, a rental truck exploded in the parking garage of the World Trade Center. The media assumed, as usual, the terrorist bombing was political, motivated by the Palestinian cause, but an Islamist shaykh was found to be the instigator. US authorities still had not realized the religiously radical sources of terrorism, even though a renewed look at the 1981 assassination of President Sadat was beginning to open eyes to the Islamist dimension that was missed at the time. The Islamists were enemies of any and all states and dedicated to the destruction of the international state system in its entirety.

I was on the thirty-eighth floor of the United Nations Secretariat Building when the World Trade Center bomb went off. The New York Police Department soon arrived to tell us the UN had been the secondary target. In that easeful era the UN parking garage was entirely unsecured, as was the Secretariat high-rise; anyone could walk in the front entrance on First Avenue and take an elevator directly to the secretary-general's floor. When UN officials heard they had been targeted they were uncomprehending, failing to understand why anyone would oppose the world organization of member states dedicated to "the maintenance of international peace and security." The idea that acts of terrorism might have a religious ideology behind them was particularly dumbfounding. The UN and the international state system were eventual products of the 1648 Treaty of Westphalia, which had established a general understanding that religion, while to be respected, must be kept out of international affairs in order to prevent the recurrence of a religious conflict such as the Thirty Years' War. That understanding worked so well for more than three centuries that the reemergence of religion in twentieth-century international affairs seemed beyond comprehension.

Similarly lacking a realization of what was now going on, the US across three presidential terms in the 1990s delivered one heedlessly pointless blow after another to the credibility and standing of the United Nations: by sending blue-helmeted peacekeepers into an ongoing war in Bosnia, where there was no peace to keep; by refusing to allow the UN even to send observers to the Dayton negotiations on the former Yugoslavia; and by launching a war for Kosovo with no reference whatsoever to the UN Security Council.

In a particularly notable effort at Arab-Israeli peace, Israel's newly elected Prime Minister Ehud Barak declared that he would take Israel's position in negotiations to its furthest possible point in order to test Palestinian seriousness. This he did in his July 2000 meeting with Clinton and Arafat at Camp David at which Israel yielded on all its long-standing "red lines"—

including its position on Jerusalem. Arafat refused even to respond, later letting it be known that had he responded to Israel in any way whatsoever he would have been done away with by Islamist radicals.

Here we can begin to realize what had been taking place in the Middle East in the decade after the Cold War: the betrayal of the Palestinian cause by the Arab states.

At this point, the only woven structure left to function for the region was the grid of states that had been dropped down upon the Middle East after the post–World War I collapse of the Ottoman Empire and caliphate. These states had endured a variety of retrograde and oppressive governments that never quite fully attained comfortable membership in the international state system, primarily owing to their failure to effectively serve the peoples under their rule. Now, in the 1990s, it was beginning to be understood that, desperate to shore up their own survival as regimes, they in fact were unraveling the fabric of their own power.

First, by welcoming the assassination of President Sadat of Egypt and then threatening King

Hussein of Jordan they had taken away the Arab state role so vital for the Palestinian cause. Then, silently, they made clear among themselves that they would fight no more controversial wars against Israel on behalf of the Palestinians, wars the Arab states had lost one after another. Instead the Arab regimes would promise the political, psychological, and material support and terror training needed for the Palestinians to violently confront Israel on their own; thus the Arab regimes expressed their willingness to go all out in fighting and dying to the last Palestinian. Underlying this momentous turnabout was the Arab state regimes' primary purpose: to preserve themselves in power by redirecting the disaffection and opposition of their own peoples toward Israel (and America) and by hyper-elevating the Palestinian cause to become the sole issue for the entire Arab-Islamic world. In fact, the Arab regimes had simply turned the Palestinian people into a protective layer of cannon fodder.

The most Machiavellian factor in this grand design was that for it to succeed, the Arab regimes had to make sure the Palestinians always failed, for only in this way could the autocrats maintain their diversionary protective shield.

It worked for a while. The regimes consolidated their rule and relieved themselves of the need to govern well.

But in the course of this vast strategic inversion, the regimes were also subsidizing and inflaming the most radically religious Islamists, those whose objectives had been steeled by the shock of the Ottoman caliphate's collapse and who now saw the possibility of overthrowing the Arab regimes themselves and ousting from the region the entire international state structure of world order. Since 1979 they had had the example of the Islamic Republic of Iran as an inspiration. Thus came Al Qaeda's declaration of war against the United States in 1996. If the far enemy—America—could be intimidated, Washington could begin to see the perils of engagement with the Middle East regimes, which, losing US support, would then become too weak to defend themselves against Islamist assault. Here in a New England university, students in the late 1990s wrote term papers analyzing Al Qaeda's declaration of war while in Washington there seemed little if any realization of its significance. Then came the acts of war launched against the World Trade Center and the Pentagon on September 11, 2001.

A TALE OF TWO PRINCES

From 9/11 into the twenty-first century it has been a tale of two princes, each interpreting from a different angle the Niebuhrian view on the challenge of world order. George W. Bush ran for the presidency promising a "humble foreign policy," sounding not unlike his presidential father's call for a "kinder, gentler" America. Then, when the 9/11 attacks occurred, Bush was suddenly a wartime president—something former President Bill Clinton mused at the time he wished he could have been.

Bush as president was undisguisedly religious and would be criticized as excessively so. His reaction to the attacks, however, could stand on its own as a classic American expression of its historically felt responsibility for the cause of world order. Secretary of State Condoleezza Rice stated Bush's reaction starkly in a major speech in Cairo: the American pursuit of stability in the Middle East at the expense of democracy had achieved neither. This was a refutation of the decades-long American realist approach to the region, standing back while the regimes governed oppressively, focused only on the flow of oil and crowd control.

Bush then announced a new American approach: First, the transformation of the greater Middle East in recognition that the region simply could not be permitted to go on as it had, in an ever-accelerating downward spiral that, if not broken, could take a vast swath of the globe's territories and peoples out of the international state system and, in doing so, undermine world order.

Second, Bush committed his administration to provide support for peoples seeking freedom and democratization in the region. This would be elaborated in Bush's second Inaugural Address as virtually an emancipation proclamation for the world, an asserted American determination to see the elimination of dictatorships around the world. This dramatic turn in US policy could be portrayed as the restoration of America's role as leader of the free world; at the same time it could be located in the long genealogy of "severe decisions" required of a prince to maintain the foundations of a stable world. Bush's 2003 decision to invade Iraq to overthrow Saddam Hussein was such a decision.

Wars in our time have been taken as opportunities for instant moralistic characterization, to serve as weapons for use in waging the political struggle.

Bush's decision on Iraq was denounced as illegal when in fact it was solidly based on over a decade of UN Security Council resolutions carrying the force of international law and passed in the cause of maintaining international peace and security in the interest of the larger necessity of world order.[9]

When the ouster of Saddam was followed by insurrection, terrorism, and the violent reemergence of the age-old Shia-Sunni conflict, Bush's decision was denounced as "the worst mistake in U.S. history" from which America might never

---

9. Charles Hill, *Trial of a Thousand Years: Islamism and World Order* (Stanford, CA: Hoover Institution Press), 89–114.

recover. But the greater significance of the US decision was twofold: First, the overthrow of the region's most odious dictator revealed to a new generation of Arab youth that they were not fated to always live under brutal oppression. The overthrow was a spark that ignited the smoldering tinder that would become the unprecedented demonstrations of the Arab Spring. Second, the US invasion lifted a rock that in Iraq, and soon elsewhere, would spew forth a seething mass of mutually antagonistic factions—ethnic, tribal, sectarian, political, cultural—that were suddenly at one another's throats. Soon it would be a war of "all against all" revealing that the generations-long narrative, incessantly promulgated by the regimes, that there was but one Arab nation in total unity and stability, beset only by the existence of Israel, had been a lie of vast proportions. Bush's decision had accelerated the eruption of a truth that had to come out.

Ideas have consequences. Bush took a "severe decision" in a lineage of thought traceable to Augustine's *City of God* in the fifth century. Bush may never have read Reinhold Niebuhr's *Moral Man and Immoral Society,* although during

Bush's student years at Yale multiple copies of the book were on the library shelves and Niebuhr's thought was much discussed among faculty and students.[10]

As outlined earlier in this essay, there are two sides to Niebuhr, most vividly revealed in his *The Irony of American History:* the necessity at extreme moments for the leader to take an action that unavoidably will transgress individual moral standards, and the arrogant and even blasphemous conduct of American leaders who fail to see the damaging consequences of their actions on the world and the country. President Bush stood on the first side of the Niebuhr fence and revalidated his decision in the face of immense adversarial political pressure when he decided in 2007 on the "surge" in US military force in Iraq.

President Barack Obama, who spoke persuasively to the press about Niebuhr's influence on him and who, in his Nobel Peace Prize speech of 2009, delivered "as thoroughly Niebuhrian an

---

10. Conversation with Professor Gaddis Smith, who taught diplomacy and foreign affairs at Yale University when George W. Bush was enrolled there.

utterance as we are ever likely to hear a sitting president utter"[11] in practice stood on the other side of the Niebuhrian dichotomy.

While Obama's Nobel Prize speech had a hardheaded pro-American tone, from the opening of his administration he indicated his belief that most of what American leaders had done for decades had been the cause of, or had worsened, the problems of the world. That being the case, then America's allies had been complicit with us and we would need to distance ourselves from them, as we did with Britain and Israel, even as we reached out to understand the legitimate concerns of those we had branded as adversaries. In Obama's early speeches, when he addressed the peoples of the world, he offered America's support for peace and stability, omitting to mention "freedom and democracy." It was soon clear that the US would step back from a leading world role. We were *not* an exceptional country; we owed apologies to many; his task as

---

11. R. Ward Holder and Peter B. Josephson, *The Irony of Barack Obama: Barack Obama, Reinhold Niebuhr and the Problem of Christian Statecraft* (Burlington, VT: Ashgate Publishing, 2012), 3, citing Hendrik Hertzberg quoting the historian William Lee Miller.

president would be to close down wars, not decide to send American forces to fight them.

And so, as the spark of freedom ignited protests in Lebanon, Iran, and then the Arab Spring, the US said nothing and did little. As the "war of all against all" spread across the region threatening American gains in Iraq and Afghanistan, as Al Qaeda Islamists made surprising gains even though the president had proclaimed them on the run, the condition of regional security and its implications for world order grew ever worse in the second decade of the twenty-first century. The Great Unraveling was under way.

That Obama may not have understood Reinhold Niebuhr in the first place may be drawn from his review of "just war" theory in his Nobel Prize speech—that war must be either "a last resort or in self-defense," or undertaken in defense of others on humanitarian grounds. In this sense, the theory is a way to *excuse* leaders from hard decisions; Niebuhr's argument was that war inherently *involves* injustice and that the prince must be strong enough in his perception of the leadership required to act nonetheless.

At the start of Obama's second presidential term, the US moved in another direction, launching a program of heightened diplomatic activity in and on the Middle East. A strong State Department team of specialists was rebuilt. But the diplomacy was naked, imperiled by credible strength. Running counter to core principles of statecraft, a peace conference was convened during an ongoing civil war in which neither side saw reason to yield. Diplomacy was pushed to the forefront when American military leverage had been ruled out and the levers of economic pressure eased; while the US encouraged regimes with long records of deceit and violations of international obligations to become normal, it remained oblivious to the radical ideological and political survival factors driving those regimes. Thus the US committed itself to a major effort to persuade the unpersuadable.

Whatever policy goals the US now hopes to achieve, American actions are in reality accommodating a major change in the concept of world order as it has been shaped over the past three hundred years or more—a universalist, procedural, human rights-based international system based on a recognition of both the doctrine of the equality of states and the legitimate status of the major powers—represented respectively by the General Assembly and Security Council of the United Nations. Instead, what can now be seen taking shape is a world retreating into old and dangerous forms of spheres of influence, each region to be dominated by a single power center: Asia from Beijing, the former Soviet empire's lands from Moscow; Europe as an arena for outside powers. And for the Middle East, the US now leans toward an acceptance of Iranian hegemony, even to the extent of a Tehran-shaped sphere of influence across the region—an outcome that is simply impossible to achieve given the religious and demographic counter-realities of the Arab-Islamic world.

Spheres of influence cannot be woven together. What is now required is "the old State-secret"— weaving: an actively engaged, omnidirectional American involvement to support and interact with whatever faction, regime, sect, leader, or state that truly seeks to gain legitimacy as a good citizen in the established international system. And in doing this, to interweave the

region with those forces outside the Middle East
who take world order and democratization seriously. There is a new narrative taking shape in
the region to take the place of the false unity,
stability, and anti-Israel narrative shattered by
America's invasion of Iraq under President Bush.
The new narrative reveals Iran and its surrogates, from Assad's Syria to Hezbollah to Hamas
and beyond, to be the enemy of world order
from a revisionist Shia source even as the resur-
gent Al Qaeda and its surrogates do the same
from a renegade Sunni source. The US must
marshal all possible elements in the region, and
supporters from without, to defeat both these
enemies of order.

As always, the highest art of strategic weaving
is not simply to gather existing strands in a coher-
ent pattern, but to do so in a way that creates a
whole that is new and greater than its parts.

And as "the old State-secret" is employed,
American leaders need to be ever so ready to
take, at the most dangerous and consequential
moments, "severe decisions."

ABOUT THE AUTHOR

CHARLES HILL, a career minister in the US Foreign Service, is a research fellow at the Hoover Institution and cochair of its Herbert and Jane Dwight Working Group on Islamism and the International Order. He was executive aide to former US secretary of state George P. Shultz (1983–89) and served as special consultant on policy to the secretary-general of the United Nations (1992–96). He is also the Brady-Johnson Distinguished Fellow in Grand Strategy and senior lecturer in international studies and in humanities at Yale University. He is the author of *Trial of a Thousand Years: World Order and Islamism* (Hoover Institution Press, 2011).

Among Hill's awards are the Superior Honor Award from the Department of State in 1973 and 1981; the Presidential Distinguished Service Award in 1987 and 1989; and the Secretary of State's Medal in 1989. He was granted an honorary doctor of laws degree by Rowan University.

HERBERT AND JANE DWIGHT
WORKING GROUP ON
ISLAMISM AND THE
INTERNATIONAL ORDER

THE HERBERT AND JANE DWIGHT WORKING GROUP ON ISLAMISM AND THE INTERNATIONAL ORDER seeks to engage in the task of reversing Islamic radicalism through reforming and strengthening the legitimate role of the state across the entire Muslim world. Efforts will draw on the intellectual resources of an array of scholars and practitioners from within the United States and abroad, to foster the pursuit of modernity, human flourishing, and the rule of law and reason in Islamic lands—developments that are critical to the very order of the international system.

The Working Group is cochaired by Hoover fellows Fouad Ajami and Charles Hill, with an active participation by Hoover Institution Director John Raisian. Current core membership includes Russell A. Berman and Abbas Milani, with contributions from Zeyno Baran, Marius Deeb, Reuel Marc Gerecht, Ziad Haider, R. John Hughes, Nibras Kazimi, Bernard Lewis, Habib C. Malik, Camille Pecastaing, Itamar Rabinovich, Lieutenant Colonel Joel Rayburn, Lee Smith, Samuel Tadros, Joshua Teitelbaum, and Tunku Varadarajan.

Freedom or Terror: Europe Faces Jihad
Russell A. Berman

The Myth of the Great Satan:
A New Look at America's Relations with Iran
Abbas Milani

Torn Country: Turkey between Secularism and Islamism
Zeyno Baran

Islamic Extremism and the War of Ideas: Lessons from Indonesia
R. John Hughes

The End of Modern History in the Middle East
Bernard Lewis

The Wave: Man, God, and the Ballot Box in the Middle East
Reuel Marc Gerecht

Trial of a Thousand Years: World Order and Islamism
Charles Hill

Jihad in the Arabian Sea
Camille Pecastaing

The Syrian Rebellion
Fouad Ajami

Motherland Lost: The Egyptian and Coptic Quest for Modernity
Samuel Tadros

Iraq after America: Strongmen, Sectarians, Resistance
Joel Rayburn

[For a list of essays published under the auspices of the
WORKING GROUP ON ISLAMISM AND THE INTERNATIONAL ORDER,
please see page ii.]

INDEX